NATIONAL GEOGRAPHIC

Ladders

TRANSFORMERS

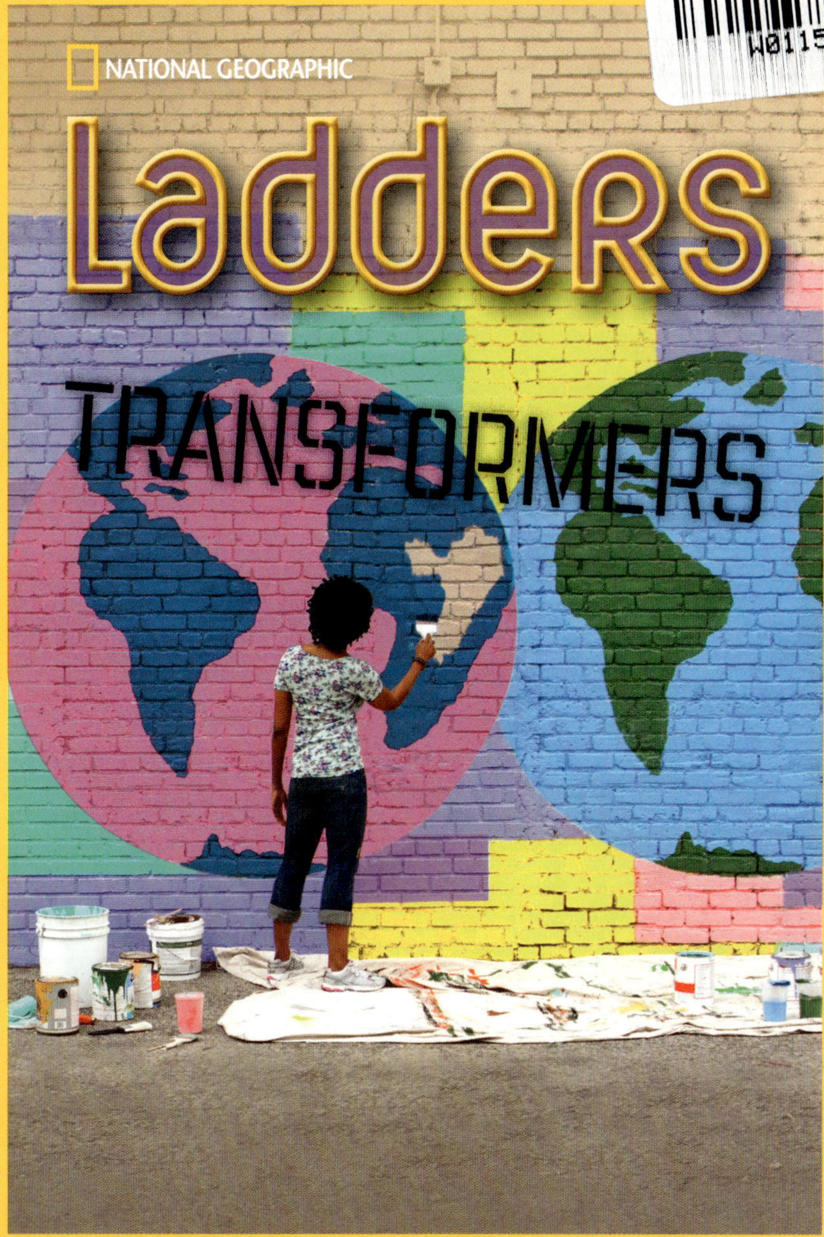

THE QUILTERS of

Think about all the things that you throw away. Could you use the materials again? In other words, could they be **"repurposed"**? If we can think of new uses for old things, we can save money.

Gee's Bend is a small town in Alabama. Many generations of women who live there have been using old clothes and cloth scraps to make quilts. The quilts are beautiful. They have bold colors and patterns. They also provide warmth in colder seasons.

GEE'S BEND

by Brigetta Christensen

What makes the quilts of Gee's Bend special? People who visited Gee's Bend saw the **artistry** in the quilters' work. The **transformation** of scraps to art in the form of useful quilts makes the quilts unique.

NECESSITY DRIVES INVENTION

The tradition of quilting in Gee's Bend, Alabama, began at the turn of the 20th century. Many people in Gee's Bend lived simply. Their homes didn't have updated heating systems. Gee's Bend is in the south, but it still gets cold. People put newspapers on their walls to keep cold air from getting inside. Men and women worked long hours on their farms. And they wore through their work clothes quickly.

Families did not have very much money. They couldn't buy blankets to keep warm. Good material was never thrown away. So quilters used scraps of cloth to make warm quilts.

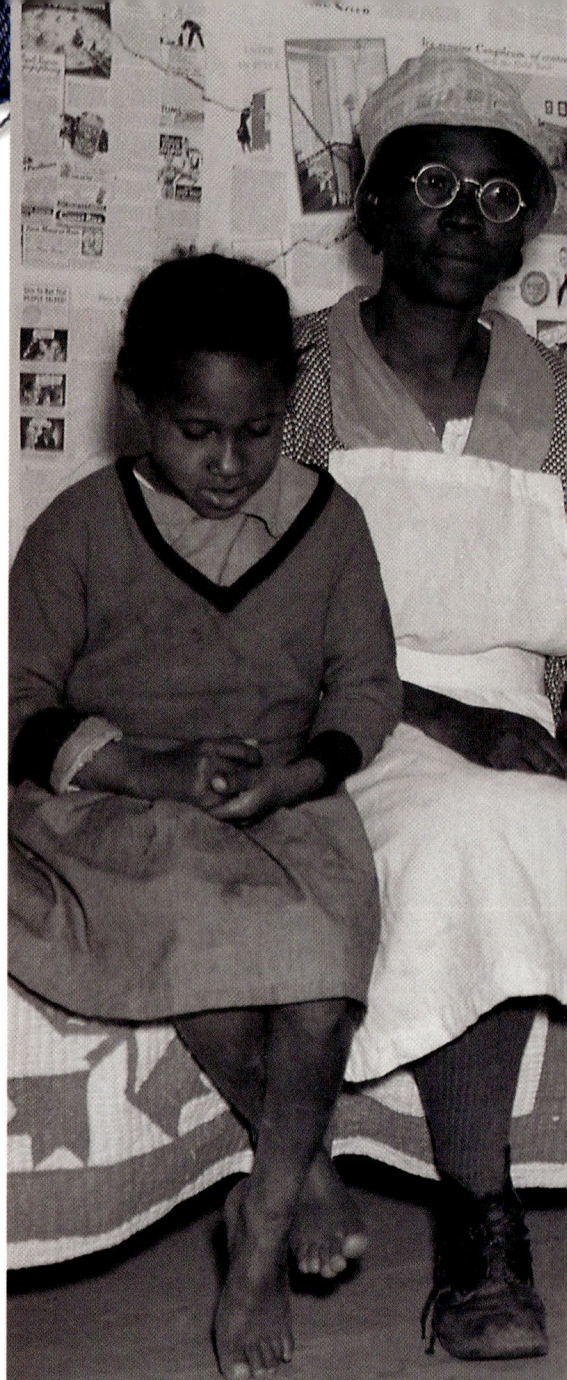

THE CRAFT OF

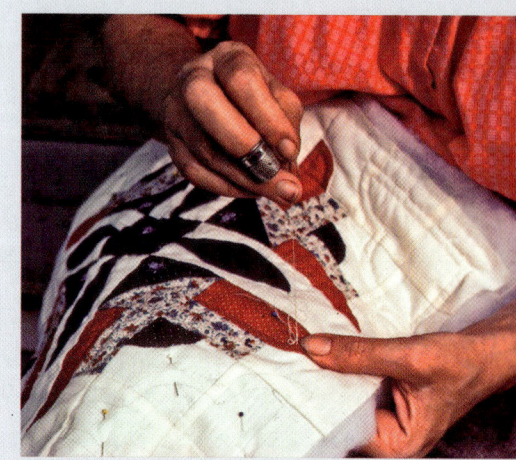

QUILTING

True quilts have three layers. They have a top layer of pieces. They have a middle layer of batting. And the back layer is called backing. Putting all three layers together is called basting. Some quilters use a form to hold the layers together as they sew. Others do not.

Today the stitching is usually done on a sewing machine. In the past, many quilters sewed by hand.

A pincushion secures pins and loose bits of thread.

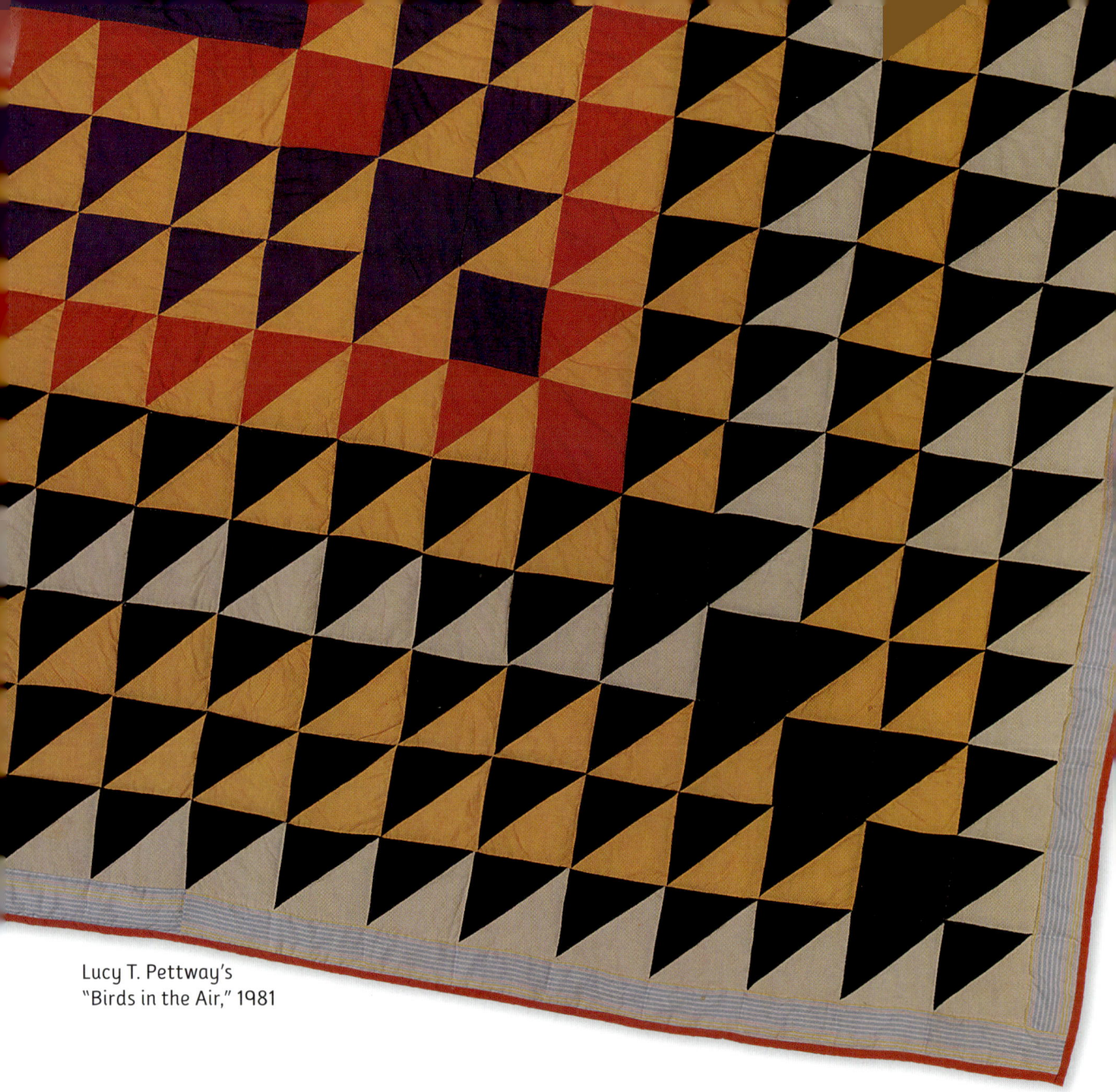

Lucy T. Pettway's
"Birds in the Air," 1981

TRANSFORMING TRADITION

In 1966, quilters in Gee's Bend formed a quilting collective, or group. It was called the Freedom Quilting Bee. Their work helped earn money for their families. It also provided a place to practice their craft.

The quilt collective was a transformation. Quilters now worked as a group. The technique of quilting also had a transformation. Young quilters created their own patterns. They did not have to follow the patterns of others.

corduroy and cotton quilt by
China Pettway, circa 1975

Arcola Pettway's "Lazy Gal," 1976

cotton quilt by Jessie T. Pettway, 1950s

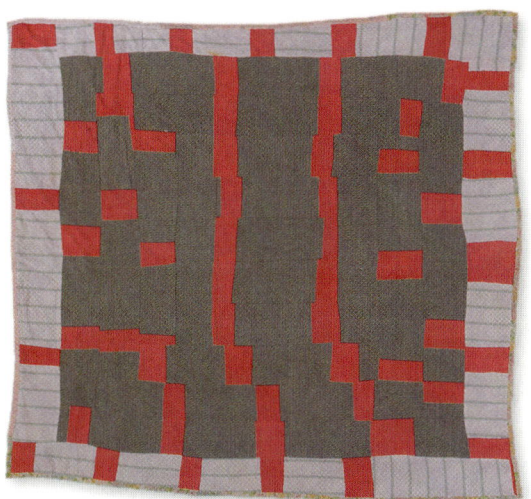

Missouri Pettway's
"Path through the Woods," 1971

Most quilters learned how to quilt from their mothers. Gee's Bend has at least six generations of quilters. They follow the traditions created by members of the Gee's Bend community. Members of the Pettway family made many of the quilts in the Quilts of Gee's Bend™ collection. They used what they learned from older family members to create their own designs.

ART OR CRAFT?

The quilters of Gee's Bend made quilts for practical reasons. But they followed a creative process. They worked in a similar way to other other artists. Their creative work and the usefulness of the quilts were both important. But at first, the quilters of Gee's Bend didn't consider how their quilts were like museum artwork. Art critics did.

Art critics thought the quilts were as good as the work of mid-20th century artists. Critics saw artistry and creativity in the Gee's Bend quilts. The quilts were like modern art paintings in many ways.

The amazing quilts of Gee's Bend became examples of mid-20th century art. Some quilt patterns have been compared to the artwork of Mark Rothko and Paul Klee. In 2002, the Museum of Fine Arts in Houston had the first exhibit of 70 quilts from Gee's Bend. And in 2003, the quilters of Gee's Bend formed a new group, The Gee's Bend Quilters Collective. They continue to make quilts.

No. 5/No. 22. 1950 (dated on reverse 1949).
Oil on canvas, 9' 9" x 8' 11 1/8" (297 x 272 cm).
Gift of the artist.

A museum curator walks through the Gee's Bend quilt exhibit. This photo shows the exhibit at the High Museum of Art in Atlanta in 2006.

These works by Mark Rothko (left) and Paul Klee (right) show bold colors. Both artists were very important in modern art movements such as abstract expressionism.

Mountain Village (Autumnal) 1934, (no 209). Oil on primed canvas on wooden panel, 2' 4 1/8" x 1' 9 1/2" (71.5 x 54.4 cm).

Nettie Young's
"Milky Way," 1971

DOING IT YOURSELF

The women of Gee's Bend passed down the tradition of quilt making. This was out of a need to repurpose the materials they had. They learned to make the things they wanted, like dresses and quilts. They learned to express themselves by making these things by hand.

Sometimes people are unable to buy new items. So they make the items by hand. It's fun to see what you can make with simple materials.

People today are coming back to the crafting traditions. They are making items by hand out of **necessity** and because it's enjoyable. They are learning how to do-it-themselves. This trend is called DIY (Do-It-Yourself). Some DIYers learn skills from family or friends. Others use the Internet for information. And the women of Gee's Bend are great examples of this kind of work. They show that simple materials can be used to create something beautiful.

Check In How did the quilters transform fabric scraps?

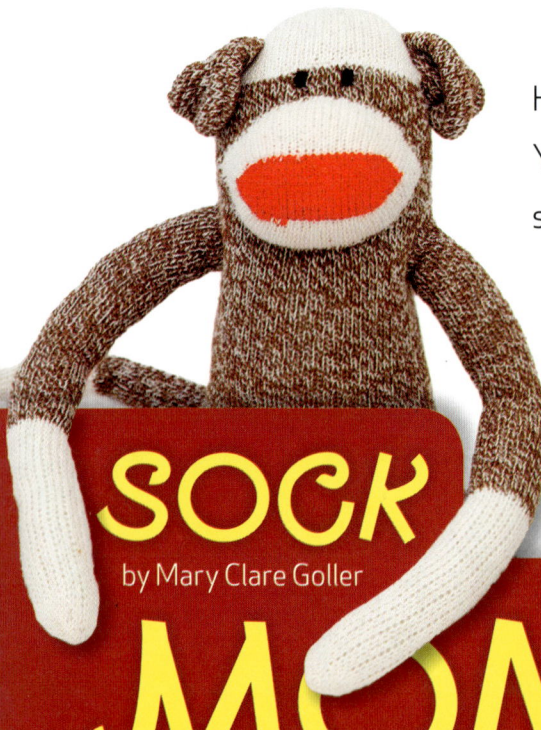

Have you ever held a soft sock monkey toy? You can **transform** old materials to make something new. Sturdy socks with red heels were first made in the 1890s. Workers wore them. Then the tradition of making sock toys began. Follow these steps to make your own sock monkey.

SOCK MONKEYS!
by Mary Clare Goller

Step 1

Turn one sock inside out. Flatten the sock with the heel centered. You will make two lines of stitches that are about $\frac{1}{2}$ inch apart, as shown in the photo. When you finish each stitch at the sock band, make a knot.

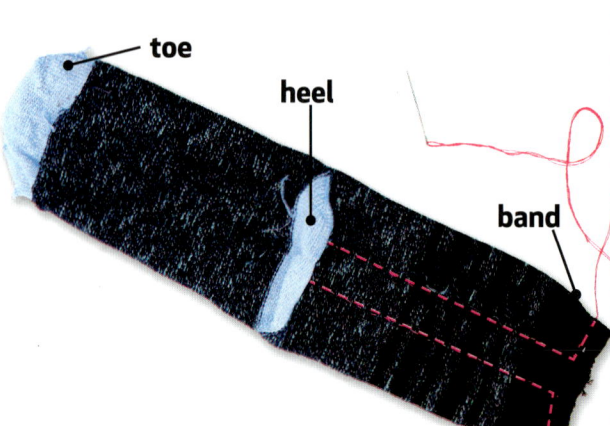

toe
heel
band

Step 2

Make a cut down the middle of the sock between the two lines of stitching. Leave an opening near the center of the heel.

back

12

Materials

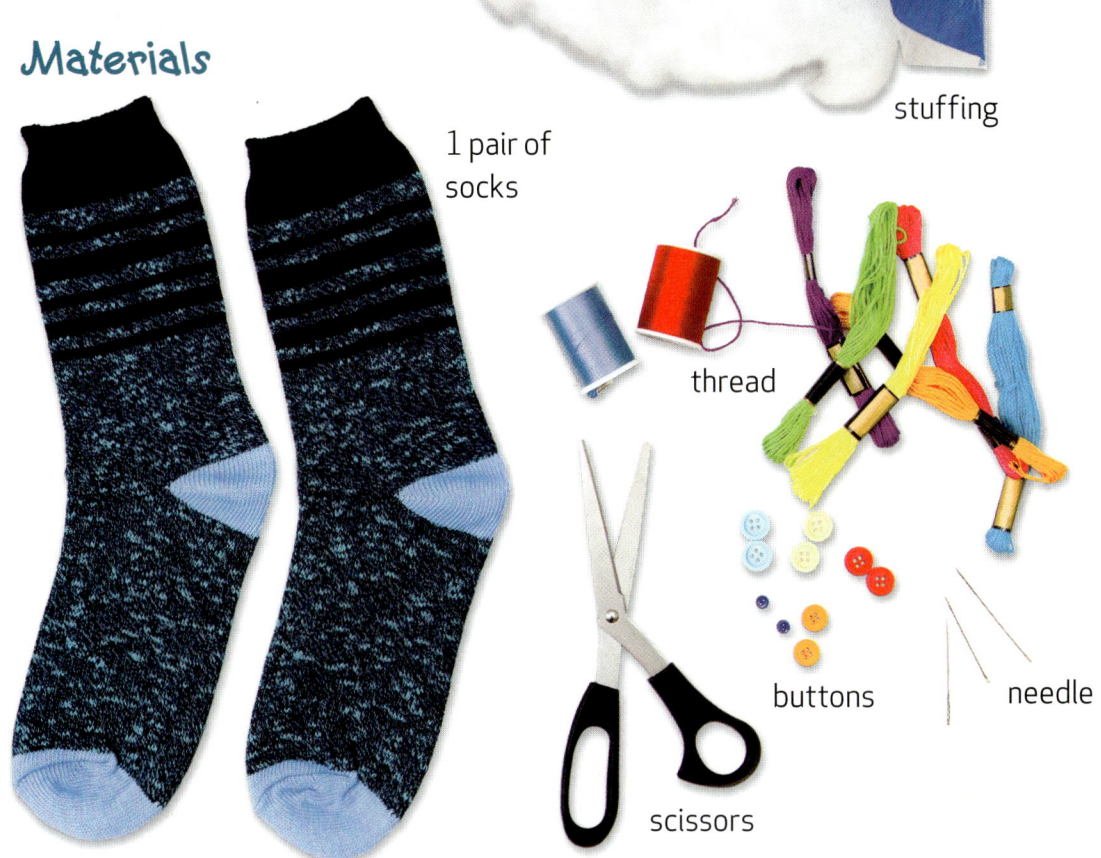

stuffing

1 pair of socks

thread

scissors

buttons

needle

Step  3

Turn the sock right side out so the stitches are inside. Stuff the sock through the opening. You will stuff the monkey's legs and upper body.

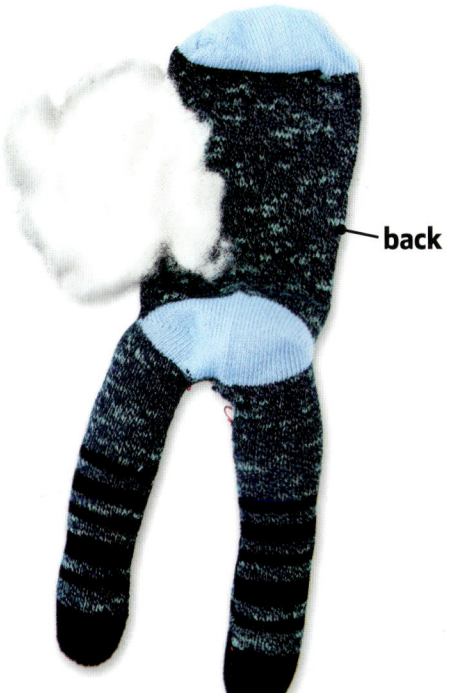

back

Step 4

Once the whole body is stuffed, sew the opening near the heel closed. You now have the monkey's body, including its head, without its mouth or ears.

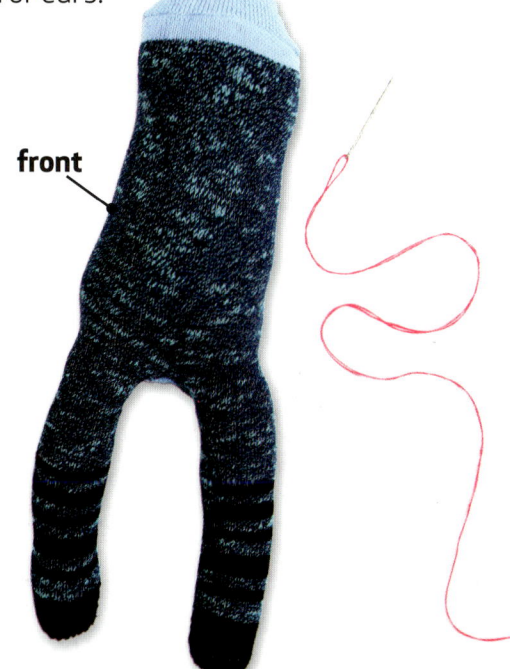

front

Turn the second sock inside out. Cut the sock apart just above the heel. Make cuts to the bottom portion of the sock for the ears, mouth and tail. You will have one small, unused part of material.

Next take the portion for the arms and stitch two straight seams about $\frac{1}{2}$ inch apart. These stitches are like the ones you made in Step 1.

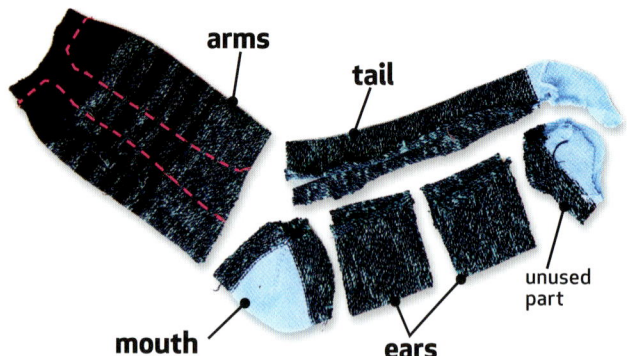

arms

tail

mouth

ears

unused part

Set the heel (mouth) aside for now. Sew a seam for the tail and stuff it. Stuff the arms. Sew around the edges of the material for each ear, leaving a small opening in order to turn ears right-side out.

Attach the ears to the top of the toy. Close up any openings as you sew. Attach the arms and tail. Sew the body parts right to the body using small, tight stitches.

Begin to attach the mouth to the face with small, tight stitches. Leave a small opening at one corner and stuff completely. Close the opening with a final stitch.

Finish your monkey with button eyes. Or sew soft eyes with thread if the toy is for a baby or toddler. Maybe even add a stitch for a belly button!

Be proud of your **handiwork.** Practice these steps more with other **repurposed** socks. You can make a whole family of monkeys!

Check In What are the materials needed to make this toy?

Urban Transformations

by Joseph Kowalski

Big cities mean a lot of people and a lot of buildings. Buildings and other structures take up open spaces. These structures and the areas around them are usually busy with activity. However, some structures can become **abandoned.** They sit empty and unused until someone thinks of a possible **transformation.** The transformation could restore or **revitalize** abandoned structures and their surroundings.

From Highway to Urban Oasis

Seoul, South Korea, is a city with a population of more than ten million. A restored habitat and river run through the heart of this city. A transformation turned an old highway area into an urban park. Now there is ground level access to the Cheonggyecheon (Chung-gye-chun) River. People can enjoy a **repurposed** part of their city. Animals and plants have also returned to this restored habitat.

Partial structures of the old highway in Seoul stand in the river.

Before construction was completed, concrete structures blocked views of cityscapes in Seoul.

An aerial view during construction

Pedestrians can now walk across the river.

How did the transformation take place? It began in 2002 and was completed quickly. Construction crews took apart the old highway. They also tore down structures that blocked the stream. The project created a lot of waste. But much of the waste was reused. The stream began to flow once again. The planners needed to think about possible floods. So the crews built barriers to prevent the river from flooding.

Planners also thought about the way the river looks. Natural plantings give the feeling of being far away from the city. The 5.84 kilometer (3.6 mile) river walk includes a waterfall, lights, and artwork. Planners included 17 access points from the city streets. People can walk from the street to the river's edge. The Cheonggyecheon restoration project gave people a place to enjoy nature in the city. And it reclaimed a natural resource of Seoul, its water. About 90,000 people visit this urban park on an average day.

Seoul's urban river walk is edged with concrete. Yet it offers a natural habitat that citizens enjoy.

Old Line, New Life

The High Line is a rail line, which sits above New York City streets. Freight trains used to run on it. The rail line had been abandoned since the 1980s. People wondered if the city would tear down the structure.

Two men who lived in the neighborhood had an idea. They wanted to transform this old landscape into a beautiful place. Now it is an above-ground park. The park stretches across miles of city neighborhoods.

This plan for transformation would save local history. It also would find a new use for the structure.

New York City has little space. So it's a good idea to reuse existing structures, like abandoned rail lines. Also it offers a beautiful route through part of the city.

An aerial view shows the abandoned rail line before reconstruction.

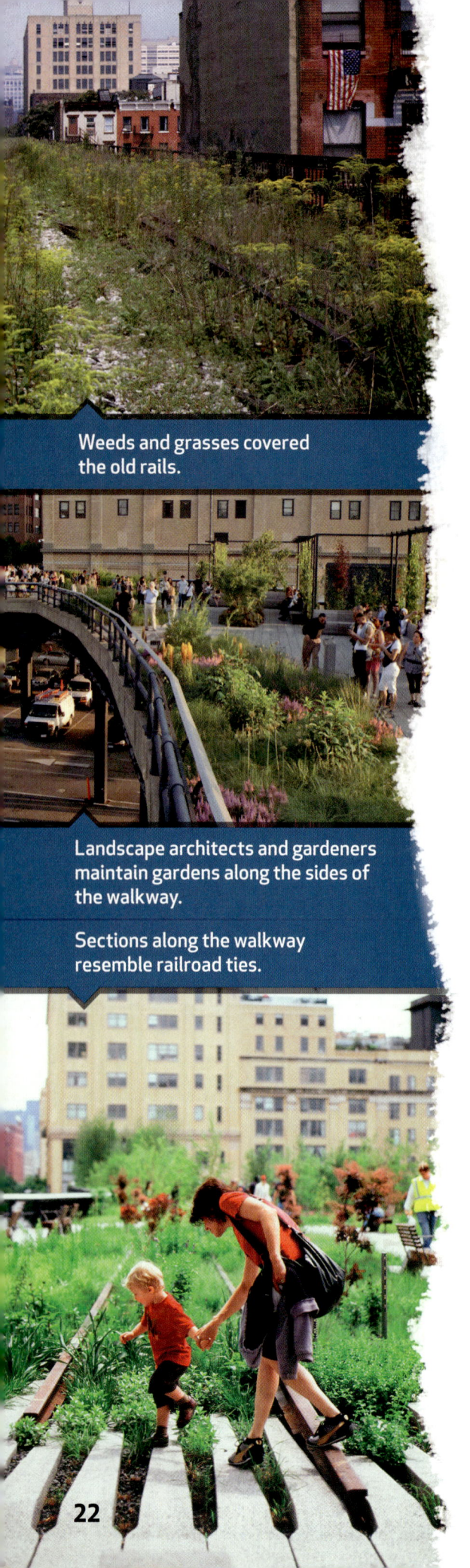

Weeds and grasses covered the old rails.

Landscape architects and gardeners maintain gardens along the sides of the walkway.

Sections along the walkway resemble railroad ties.

How was it done? The High Line was overgrown with wildflowers and weeds. The wild growth gave planners an idea. The Promenade Plantée in Paris, France also gave them an idea. It was created from abandoned rail lines, too.

Designers competed to get the job of park planners. Winning planners built the park to include original features of the track. Features like the old railway ties were left in place.

The project began in 2006 and is still in process. The High Line has become one of New York's biggest new tourist attractions. The city and the designers combined nature and planning to create a beautiful space.

In cities around the world, abandoned structures can become a revitalized space. These spaces are places to enjoy and recall local history.

Check In   What remained the same and what changed in Seoul and New York City?

23

Discuss Information

1. What connections can you make among the three pieces in *Transformers*? How are the pieces related?

2. What does it mean to be a transformer? Use information from each selection to answer this question.

3. "The Quilters of Gee's Bend" and "Urban Transformations" tell about different types of problems and solutions related to transforming old into new. What are some of the problems and solutions?

4. What would you still like to know about the people or projects in Gee's Bend, Seoul, or New York City?